AN ENGLISH SAMPLER
New and Selected Poems

AN ENGLISH SAMPLER
New and Selected Poems

Fred D'Aguiar

Chatto & Windus
LONDON

Published by Chatto & Windus 2001

2 4 6 8 10 9 7 5 3 1

Copyright © Fred D'Aguiar 2001

This page should be read in conjunction with the acknowledgements on
page 150

Fred D'Aguiar has asserted his right under the Copyright, Designs
and Patents Act 1988 to be identified as the author of this work

First published in Great Britain in 2001 by
Chatto & Windus
Random House, 20 Vauxhall Bridge Road,
London SW1V 2SA

Random House Australia (Pty) Limited
20 Alfred Street, Milsons Point, Sydney,
New South Wales 2061, Australia

Random House New Zealand Limited
18 Poland Road, Glenfield,
Auckland 10, New Zealand

Random House South Africa (Pty) Limited
Endulini, 5A Jubilee Road, Parktown 2193, South Africa

The Random House Group Limited Reg. No. 954009

A CIP catalogue record for this book
is available from the British Library

ISBN 0 7011 6711 4

Papers used by Random House are natural,
recyclable products made from wood grown in sustainable forests.
The manufacturing processes conform to the environmental
regulations of the country of origin.

Typeset by Deltatype Limited, Birkenhead, Merseyside
Printed and bound in Great Britain by
Mackays of Chatham PLC

For Matthew, Cameron, Elliot, Christopher and Nicholas

AN ENGLISH SAMPLER

A roof caves in,
      into a yard,
a yard losing
      its roof, a high
walled yard, we call
      this yard our country.

We're safe in there
      until we find
ourselves dodging
      blocks of concrete
that disintegrate
      on impact on concrete.

We can't climb those
      walls, we won't be
valiant and
      try, not in the
company of
      such young people.

So in assessment
      we praise youth,
the resilience
      thereof, the way
they are prepared
      to fall and bounce

right back up again
      while we ruminate
on possible
      pitfalls that
await us and
      befall us anyway.

To youth for showing
	how to walk away
from the knock-on
	effect of the
knock on the head
	or to the heart

or broken bones,
	this is England,
though it could be
	anywhere. We are
not herders but
	teachers. We mend

the bones and soothe
	the broken heads,
tell those big hearts
	the hurt will lessen.
The roof we crossed
	to get this far

threatened to cave
	in under us
even as we crawled
	along shadows
judged to be steel
	rafters, in pairs,

scraping our bellies,
	hands and knees on
anti-climb paint
	and praying that
those kids, our kids,
	won't see us now.

CONTENTS

From *Mama Dot*

MAMA DOT

Born on a Sunday
in the kingdom of Ashante

Sold on Monday
into slavery

Ran away on Tuesday
cause she born free

Lost a foot on Wednesday
when they catch she

Worked all Thursday
till her head grey

Dropped on Friday
where they burned she

Freed on Saturday
in a new century

ORACLE MAMA DOT

I am seated at her bare feet.
The rocking chair on floorboards
Of the veranda is the repeated break
Of bracken underfoot. *Where are we heading?*

Who dare speak in these moments before dark?
The firefly threads its infinite morse;
Crapauds and crickets are a mounting cacophony;
The laughter of daredevil bats.

Dusk thickens into night.
She has rocked and rocked herself to sleep.
She may hold silence for another millennium.
I see the first stars among cloud.

ANGRY MAMA DOT

I

She gesticulates and it's sheet lightning on our world.
Our ears cannot be stopped against her raised voice.
All the crying we ever did is a roof, soaked through.
With no gaps for thought, we save the night trembling
A string of prayers in gibberish for her rage to quell.

II

The powdery collisions of moths round a lamp.
Us, out first thing, upturned face and palm.
So her peace comes. We stick close, watching.
Busy and humming with it, she throws us clean.
I am years later fighting to break my fall.

OBEAH MAMA DOT

(her remedies)

I

I am knotted in pain.
She measures string
From navel to each nipple.

She kneads into my belly
Driving the devil
Out of my enforced fast.

II

For the fevers to subside,
I must drink the bush
Boiled to a green alluvium,

In one headback slake;
And return to bounding around,
Side-stepping bushes for days.

III

A head-knock mushrooms
Into a bold, bald,
Softened bulb.

Her poultice filled
At the end of a rainbow –
The sun above Kilimanjaro;

The murderous vial drawn,
Till the watery mound
Is a crater in burnt ground.

IV

Our rocking-chair counsellor:
Her words untangling us
from bramble and plimpler notions

Into this sudden miles-clearing.

MAMA DOT'S FOOD ALLEGORY

She's in the throes of an original quarrel:
The on/off labrish of lids,
Stirred by wooden spoons
Gaffing on rims and the fire's cackle.

We'd notice our mouths
Watering: how it comes
Is like a tune in a wind
From miles hummed all day.

And every time I am amazed
To see every plate heaped
To satisfaction, knowing more
And more the workings of that first

Combine Harvester, gathering rice
In neat bales; a job she saw
To the last grain, when all we did
Was burrow in a house of hay

Or race in paddy bags
Emptied to our fill.
We were her shoots
Sweetening with her care.

Might she have loved
The potato, dug as it is
Caked in mud, roots stubby,
Hardly knowing the sun?

So many bare-faced
Reminders of our destiny.
Sent like offerings from the dead
To pass as food, not turds.

MAMA DOT'S EXCLUSIVE

'Don't ask questions, you only get answers.'

She, doubled over a scrubbing-board;
His *hide me*, hardly out before the ignorant
Stampede across the bridge at the front yard.
Her *behind the stove*, a kiss he plants
On her parted lips in a hurry. They get
There demanding him even as her
Hands dip into the washing, ink as wet
On their search warrant; its signature
Forged with the remoteness of a jet's.

She has him breathing in for a pleated skirt,
Trying high heels like his first steps again;
Its neat folds will disguise a rip that hurt
As he ducked through barbed wire in rain;
Its hem muddied by fields of tall grass.
Take him as drawn to an oasis of light,
This guest-house plumb in the wilderness;
Its running ad reads, *NO DISTANCE TO THE
    AIRPORT* . . .
Unsure why he signed *De'ath* at the empty desk.

Having helped himself to skull-shaped keys,
He finds the bedroom like his own;
Too tired to remove make-up he was pleased
Carried him as far as the fenced zone
Their volley of shots pinged sparks off.
His head touches a blank pillowcase,
A last thought circles like a helicopter
Over a demo spilling out of a square:
How it suits like a coffin or he in her.

MAMA DOT'S TREATISE

Mosquitoes
Are the fattest
Inhabitants
Of this republic.

They suck our blood
From the cradle
And flaunt it
Like a fat wallet.

They form dark
Haloes; we spend
Our outdoors
Dodging sainthood.

They force us
Into an all-night
Purdah of nets
Against them.

O to stop them
Milking us
Till we are bait
For worms;

Worms that don't
Know which way
To turn and will
Inherit the earth.

MAMA DOT WARNS AGAINST AN EASTER RISING

Doan raise no kite is good friday
but is out he went out an fly it
us thinking maybe dere wont be a breeze
strong enouf an widout any a we to hole it
fo him he'd neva manage to get it high-up
to de tree top ware de wind kissin
de ripess sweetess fruit we cawn reach
but he let out some string bit by bit
tuggin de face into de breeze
coaxin it up all de time takin a few steps back
an it did rise up bit by bit till de lang tail
din't touch de groun an we grip de palin
we head squeeze between to watch him
an trace its rise rise rise up up up in de sky
we all want to fly in like bird but can only kite
fly an he step back juss as we beginnin
to smile fo him envy him his easter risin
when bap he let out a scream leggo string
an de kite drop outta de sky like a bird
a sail down to de nex field an we runnin to him
fogetting de kite we uncle dem mek days ago
from wood shave light as bird bone
paper tin like fedder an de tongue o kite
fo singin in de sky like a bird an de tail
fo balance string in de mout like it pullin
de longess worm an he a hole him foot
an a bawl we could see seven inch a greenheart
gone in at de heel runnin up him leg
like a vein he groanin all de way to de haspital
on de cross-bar a bike ridden by a uncle
she not sayin a word but we hearin her
fo de ress a dat day an evry year since
doan raise no kite is good friday
an de sky was a birdless kiteless wait fo her word

MAMA DOT LEARNS TO FLY

Mama Dot watched reels of film
Of inventor after inventor trying to fly.
She's so old, she's a spectator in some.

Seeing them leap off bridges straight
Into rivers, or burn
Strapped to backfiring rockets,

Or flap about with huge wings
Only to raise a whole heap of dust,
Makes her cringe: what conviction!

How misguided. Right then, she wants
To see an ancestor, in Africa; half-way
Round the world and back through time.

Her equipment's straightforward,
Thought-up to bring the lot
To her: *Come, leh we gaff girl.*

LETTER FROM MAMA DOT

I

Your letters and parcels take longer
And longer to reach us. The authorities
Tamper with them (whoever reads this
And shouldn't, I hope jumby spit
In dem eye). We are more and more
Like another South American dictatorship,
And less and less a part of the Caribbean.
Now that we import rice (rice that used
To grow wild!), we queue for most things:
Flour, milk, sugar, barley, and fruits
You can't pick anymore. I join them
At 5 a.m. for 9 o'clock opening time,
People are stabbing one another for a place
And half the queue goes home empty-handed,
With money that means next to nothing.
Every meal is salt-fish these days; we even
Curry it. Send a box soon. Pack the basics:
Flour, for some roti; powdered milk;
And any news of what's going on here.
No luxuries please, people only talk, shoes
Can wait till things improve (dey bound
Fe improve cause dem cawn get no worse!)
Everybody fed-up in truth; since independence
This country hasn't stopped stepping back;
And if you leave you lose your birthright.
With all the talk of nationality we still hungry.
Neil has joined the forces against all advice.
He brings home sardines saved from his rations
For our Sunday meal; he wears the best boots
In town. The fair is full of prizes
We threw out in better days and everyone wins
Coconuts. I wouldn't wish this on anyone,
But it's worse somehow without you here.
Write! We feast on your letters.

II

You are a traveller to them.
A West Indian working in England;
A Friday, Tonto, or Punkawallah;
Sponging off the state. Our languages
Remain pidgin, like our *dark, third,*
Underdeveloped world. I mean, their need
To see our children cow-eyed, pot-bellied,
Grouped or alone in photos and naked,
The light darkened between their thighs.
And charity's all they give: the cheque,
Once in a blue moon (when guilt's
A private monsoon), posted to a remote
Part of the planet they can't pronounce.
They'd like to keep us there.
Not next door, your house propping-up
Theirs; your sunflowers craning over
The fence, towards a sun falling
On their side; begonias that belong
To them shouldering through its tight
Staves; the roots of both mingling.
So when they skin lips to bare teeth
At you, remember it could be a grimace
In another setting: the final sleep
More and more of us meet in our prime,
(Your New Cross fire comes to mind);
Who dream nowadays of peace.
You know England, born there, you live
To die there, roots put down once
And for all. Drop me a line soon,
You know me. *Neva see come fo see.*

CARNIVAL MAMA DOT

She stands high as the gable.
Her dreadlocks house a nothingness.
Her floorlength dress is a full sail.
She leans and earth shifts its axis,
Straight, she's the world stoodstill.
Her several hearts beat as one;
Her following dance past pain;
One appears to flaunt a flung coin –
A taunt before the lightning swoop
That has it scooped in a palm
Which never fails under her spell.

Her head at the window crowds hiding places,
Fills all space with screams;
She drowns them as she passes.
By the time we are brave enough to look,
She is seen still blotting out the sun,
Still her sound makes the ground tremble.
She leaves a hazy, shucked landscape,
Where only a humming-bird flashes from cover,
Sticks momentarily in mid-air and is gone;
Then her dust, like the impossible Atlantic-cross
Made by the Sahara, refuses to settle.

THE DAY MAMA DOT TAKES ILL

The day Mama Dot takes ill,
The continent has its first natural disaster:
Chickens fall dead on their backs,
But keep on laying rotten eggs; ducks upturn
In ponds, their webbed feet buoyed forever;
Lactating cows drown in their sour milk;
Mountain goats lose their footing on ledges
They used to skip along; crickets croak,
Frogs click, in broad daylight; fruits
Drop green from trees; coconuts kill travellers
Who rest against their longing trunks;
Bees abandon their queens to red ants,
And bury their stings in every moving thing;
And the sun sticks like the hands of a clock
At noon, drying the very milk in breasts.

Mama Dot asks for a drink to quench her feverish thirst:
It rains until the land is waist-deep in water.
She dreams of crops being lost: the water drains
In a day leaving them intact. She throws open her window
To a chorus and rumpus of animals and birds,
And the people carnival for a week. Still unsteady
On her feet, she hoes the grateful ashes
From the grate and piles the smiling logs on it.

FAREWELL MAMA DOT

I

I'd approach unseen
Along a hair's breadth
Perpendicular to the tsetse's
Tail, the pilot's-cockpit head
Bobbing in a coasting breeze.

Tied to string,
It circled all day
As if stacked, forgotten,
In airport cloud
And fuelled there.

Vaccines, tongue-worried
Fillings, a metal taste,
Overlapping announcements,
Crisp turnstiles,
Beginning insects at dusk.

My iron concentration
Before lassoing it,
Modelled this flight;
I piloted a cotton trail
Then, to finish seated

For five thousand miles,
On unfurling vapour.
The brittle, ornate tsetse
Stomaching better than me
A blind change of climate.

II

Her rocker halted,
Is earth's spin lost.

Her stripped bed,
Our world become savannah.

Her coffin dances down
Six feet to a wailing chorus.

Her shovelling over
Scores on greenheart, amplified;

Her ground rising-up oh Jah,
From sweet diminuendo to bass.

Her rounding off by delicate pats
With the backs of shovels.

Her new-made bed of flowers.
That second shadow *is she*.

TOWN-DADDY

For Donald D'Aguiar

Friday afternoons the national bus from Georgetown
Pulls up alongside the bridge at the front of the house
And is overtaken by sand, rain-cloud heading further inland.

We are there to greet it, one hand waves, one shades the eyes,
Edging right back from the road as it draws near,
Until we are perched on the parched lips of the trench.

Town-daddy in sandals with their fat leather strips
Criss-crossing, steps down as if testing the coolness of water,
The firmness of ground he can call his as far as sight.

He brings enough parcels for everyone to carry something,
Our neat O keeps swing-room for his walking-stick.
His sandal creaks as his heel rises and his weight pivots now

On the ball of one foot. There is the settling and unsettling
Of logs laid side by side as the entire cavalcade cross
Into the yard's cricket-pitch path, left of the stunted guinep,

To the porch. Hear the bus pick up, changing gears
Well into double figures as it mounts to the interior.
We lead him ducking through half-doors, three steps to mind.

What's always too soon is him making for the capital, so deep
Below sea-level that liners rear up from the brimming water
Like fabulous ships of the air to land way in the sky.

PAPA-T

For Reginald Messiah

When Grandad recited the Tennyson learned at sea,
I saw companies of redcoats tin-soldiering it
Through rugged country, picked-off one by one
By poison-tipped blow-darts or arrows from nowhere:
Their drums' panicky rattle, their bugler's yelp,
Musket-clap and popping cannons, smoke everywhere.

He'd cut short to shout, *If yu all don't pay me mind,*
I goin ge yu a good lickin an sen yu to bed, resuming
As he breathed in, his consonants stretched past recall,
Into a whales' crying place, beginning polyp kingdoms,
Shipwrecked into Amerindian care for months. We'd sit tight,
All eyes on our sweet seasalter, for that last-line-sound,

Someone mistimed once, making him start again.
These days the perfect-lined face of a blank page,
Startles at first, like Papa-T's no-nonsense recitals;
It has me itching to bring him reeling-off in that tongue –
Honour the charge they made! Honour the Light Brigade,
Noble six hundred: to hear, to disobey.

MASQUERADE

His passage of time is a series of dustclouds.
Streets widen at the end of town
Into sheer savannah, rolled bundles of bracken.

He watches a crow dip its beak and imagines
A living quill as its head throws back to swallow.

His Cadillac is a well-kept secret
Plunged thirty feet to the bottom of this ravine.
The steering-wheel has him jacked to plush upholstery.

It's a B-road past disused miles of track
Running deep into exhausted mines.

As a child he skipped those sleepers
Or lay in wait for Black Boy, the daily steam-express,
To flatten a six-inch nail into a knife.

It left a thick smoke trail that swept
Rice-paper-thin over ripening paddy.

It whistled at the crossroads where a woman
And child in a cart were carried
A quarter of a mile up the track.

He fished his brother out of a gully, found the mule
Grazing; his mother, no memory would want to account for.

Before a fit the skinned spider-monkeys
Failed to cure, he smells cut-grass and sees purple,
And a train, approaching his ear on the line.

ON DUTY

Gun-metal is somehow cool even in this heat.
They press the cherished barrels to their cheeks
From time to time. Little else is done,
Nothing said, except to blow down the neck
Of uniforms or peer into the sight of a rifle.

It sharpens a wavering landscape under the nose,
And the capillaries of a browned, dust-caked leaf;
Including a man's lean, guarded figure, stepping clear
Of trees; whose bare soles seem to skip along
The steamy bitumen-road, with hardly a touch.

It's a fragrance he loves, recalling days
When the giant Barber-Green unrolled its linoleum
Through the heart of this country.
It's a sight they have waited for all morning,
Beaten by this hottening monument hoisted now

To its zenith; rehearsing the features of this man,
Sure to come hot-stepping it to quench his thirst
At the official tap on the town's pipeline.
They have him lie face-down on the bonnet
Of a patrol car; it's a brand's warmth;

Its windscreen wipers poised on a dusty arc.
The engine's steady pulse drowns his own,
For it churrs and churrs, churning this memory
Like a broken record: how in broad daylight
They ordered three he knew to do press-ups

Till exhausted, then to run, barely able to break
Out of tottering before the guns blazed;
Giving his name as witness in the heat of it all,
And now this: a pistol to his head, they fire
An instruction, *Bwoy, we goin ge yu a chance, run!*

FEEDING THE GHOSTS

A solid absence, picturing the lost gold
Of El Dorado; the ruins of Great Zimbabwe.

A sudden shudder like the dive of mercury
Escaping a thermometer through minus.

The legs are the grassy brink of a precipice;
The kerosene-wick of a lamp kindles a volcano.

A tropical night, yet windows open wide
Cannot draw any of a thousand insects in.

Generations of dust, in floorboard creases, stir.

GUYANESE DAYS

As a child I worked this land half-naked,
Growing into patched, taken-in clothes.
It was one crop alongside another
For miles; tree-lined boundaries;
Paths wavering deep into shrubbery
Breaking onto clearings, far as the eye.

I used to sit and count the coconuts crash
Down: one this minute, two the next;
They skidded off branches, bounced trunks
To bang neat grooves in the mud, splash
Ponds or rolling, they'd come higgledy
Piggledy to nestle at my shaded spot.

Now I shake a Downs-tree bending ripe,
My head bent as its marble-sized fruits
Come showering in the first, huge drops
Of a downpour, my shirt held-up to load,
Eating a few choice ones in between;
Straightening to spit the seed far.

The balls of my feet dodge splintery
Plimplers as I pick up the dust track
Home, having to shoo the winged, stinging
Marabunta from my catch, tongue turning
A seed until smoothed white, humming
A tune that woke with me today.

Morning-school is a nursery rhyme
Sung till learned by heart, even tables,
So recall is an easy melody found whole;
This time Anancy tricks his wife and four
Children into each giving him half
Their share from a hard-won hand of bananas.

The pen was no fishing-rod made from a branch
Broken and shaped with a nail, my train-crushed
Knife, and dangled over fresh water, waiting
For the cork to dip, the worm still wriggling
On the zinc hook, its tip fanned to bite
Against pull, water creeping up the twine.

Once the bait took it dipped expanding circles.
The pen was harder to hold than the slingshot:
Limbs combed for the perfect fork, shaved
Of bark to gleam, two rubber bands strapped
Uppermost on the V and straddled by a tongue
For holding rounded, sun-baked clay.

The pen fought the push and pull of muscles:
Tsetse perched on a fence, my approach made
All afternoon, weight pivoted over the last
Inches, outstretched arm and the tail pincered
Between index finger and thumb, tied to string
And flown till boredom cut it loose or providence.

The blank page had no tale to tell:
What animal by its clover paw-print
Dared to cross the yard last night,
Losing itself once more to infinite
Pasture; where best to lay gum for birds
To light on and be caged; when rain.

Empty page gave eye-watering glare in sunshine.
Filling it – the nonsensical muddying of water
That squanders the gift of an afternoon swim;
Slingshot dropping short of ripest fruit.
Pen and page were like hoe and stony ground;
A full-moon smothered by reams of cloud.

The rhyme fell from my lips a thousand feet
Onto line slate: coconut-husk stripped
On a half-sunken metal rod – such veined,
Bloodless flesh ripping with a hoarse cry;
Uprooting the shoots false-named 'growee'
For their sugary heart, mangroves were downed.

Left-handed, my knuckles whitened around the pen,
Punctured the page, broke pencil-leads
Sharpened to stubbles running into miles
Of capital and common letters. Long before Z
I was sure it would come to zilch without teacher
To guide my hand, they slanted and buckled.

I dreamed through these afternoon exercises.
I'd find a shaded spot and see the way clouds
Form animals and demonic faces in blustering outlines.
They paraded my field of vision in a wind-blown
Trajectory of portraits and profiles. Anywhere
But facing the blackboard, flies warring

Among fine, stubborn, orbiting chalk-dust,
Wild cane swing hurtling it, the flies disbanded.
Or dodging my shadow: cast ahead one moment,
Following the next or lost under foot.
Grass tickling my instep, I'd pull up clumps
Between my clenched toes, the last stretch

To the shell pond dashed headlong,
The merest pause at the brink to kick off
My khaki short-pants and a smarting belly-splash
That touched sand. The chalk-caked morning
Cleared with deep breaths, the rhythm of dive
After dive and the pen's zig-zag recedes, recedes.

Drag then the feet in small steps in silence
Back to newly thickening chalk-dust, to flies
Battling and teacher in front of class
In the same starched manner as if riveted
There all through lunch, flexing the cane
Into a bow or straight as an arrow with whistling flicks.

Pen and paper looked even glummer after noon.
They did teacher's every bidding like pets.
They felt like tools not held before,
Each letter a wringing of near-dry clothes,
Their joining a jolt of needle into finger;
Thimble-thoughts of the shell pond comforting.

Collected papers and pens stacked in airless,
Musty cupboards at the end of what seems like an age.
By now, chalk-dust solid in the sunbeams, the flies
Multiplied in the space above sir's desk and mine
Fast become a graveyard of row upon row
Facing their single, dustered headstone.

The run home: Terylene unbuttoned
Shirt-tail flying in a cooler breeze
And the paling fence I had to slip sideways
Through after working one loose stave up
To double the gap, headfirst then the rest
Follows easily, left straight as a sentry.

For I am about the yard in search of parts:
A truck from two cans halved by twisting,
Made wheels, with a stick long as my leg
Nailed to a string-steered axle that broke
Out of control when we raced invisible circuits
Raising dust till the cricket and cicada cried dusk.

Or tractor from an empty spool, each tooth
Of its threaded wheels cut one by one in its edges.
It climbed everywhere powered by a wound rubber band
On a lever pulled between a pierced piece of candle.
Or a game of hop-scotch: squares drawn on ground
Pitch-clean, a dry mango seed for kicking,

Thrown and retrieved by hopping on one foot
Throughout. There'd be cheers and boos,
The index finger whipped against middle finger
And thumb, and the long, astonished whistle
At the accurate jab, the return hop heavy,
Burning; over the start-line was earth scaled.

Dusk's half-light thickening into pitch-night,
Batting till the boundary closed to the crease
Almost, flanked by house and road, having to stroke
The wooden ball under the veranda for four, fielding
On my stomach there; six if the paling's cleared;
Always lashing out for runs, fast; or making a catch.

A half-calabash used to scoop water
Fetched in a bucket for a wash, the last of it
Poured by anyone nearby, the breeze goose-pimpling.
A buttonless shirt, knotted; a baggy trouser pinned;
The day's one cooked meal downed, grouped round
The gas lamp I so loved to pump, bright.

The calabash lived green and soft, its brain-grey
Insides scraped; it dried to a stiff, malleable
Gourd, perfect for years in the mud-oven kitchen
Where enamel flaked, iron dented, copper stained,
The hand-print wore away like the floorboards;
Then cracking like the bones of a septuagenarian.

The full moon rose and a million stars . . .
All gathered to watch how its lustre creams the sky
And is sometimes lost to cloud; all begged my fisted,
Frustrated hand 'say'. I took pen between middle
And index fingers as always, page at a slant.
The moon ducked clear of clouds into this vast opening

A shooting star's exact brightness shedded everywhere;
Across two hundred yards of pasture the shell pond's
Wind-pleated water for who could skip flat stones
The most; the tang of tamarind in the air, on the tongue;
That country under the moon's phosphorescence
Was vacant papyrus, my defining sight, its calligraphy.

From *Airy Hall*

AIRY HALL

The red sand road, houses well back,
Trees there to collect dust
Whipped by traffic and flung at them,
The log bridge I am forever crossing
For a sound logs make as they shuffle
Underfoot, the lop-sided main gate
That has to be lifted into place,
Palings you can swing up and duck
Sideways through if loose and if known,
Tsetse flies stickled on their spikes
We take all afternoon approaching,
Just to pincer the papery tails
Between the thumb and index finger:
How many pushed off those tips
Leaving us all open and mannered,
As I am left now, now and always.

AIRY HALL, FIRST LIGHT

When asleep, my back
To Airy Hall's first light,
Every corner faced takes
A mirror's silvered edge
Flashed and flashed at me.

When I fasten my lids,
A thick dark is punctured
By stars; when I surrender
The stars become flowers;
When the flowers are thrown

They sprout doves,
Doves that arc fluently
Back to my clasp:
Star, flower and dove,
Bring me the light I love.

AIRY HALL BARRIER

Many deny what we see
Has anything to do with anything:
The imperialist who will not let us forget;
The runner crossing the city ahead of taxis;
Fireflies whose phosphorus belongs everywhere.

I follow the sound to a door,
One that opens on approach
To my room in water,
Pooled and swirling as if plunged
From a falls: Kaieteur.

Water sounding again,
This time a cliff-face,
Scaffold and men blasting rock
To the year of nought;
Somehow the sonic genius of a bat,

To stay latched to that sound
And find the true falls.

AIRY HALL, MID-MORNING

Sun liquefies
Reinforced glass,
Even allowing for refraction,
The staggering effect of blinds,
Mesmerizing fans and soft drinks,
Bakes to discolorations
You and your things.

Someone revs a tractor
Left idle or turning over long;
Fumes take time to ride the stillness;
The incense stick you burn
Hoping to drown them is strong,
A strength that wrestles free
The volley of sneezes you must do,

Never one or two.
All this at the lights through amber,
Green and amber again,
Rapt in last night's talk
Which grew into sweeter things:
Waking still inside her and she woken
As you withdraw and roll on your side.

AIRY HALL ICONOGRAPHY

The Tamarind hangs its head,
stings the eyes with its breath.

The Mango traps the sun by degrees,
transforms its rays into ambrosia.

The Coconut's perfect seal lets in rain,
bends with solid milk and honey.

The Guava is its own harvest,
each seed bound in fleshy juice.

The Guinep's translucence is all yours
if you skin its lips, chew its seed for the raw.

The Stinking-toe might be lopped off a stale foot,
on the tongue it does an about-turn: myrrh.

The Paw-paw runs a feather along your nose,
you want it to stop, you want more.

The Sour-sop's veneer is the wasp
treading air at the vaulted honeycomb.

The Sapodilla ducks you twice in frankincense,
you are fished out fighting to go down a third time.

The house added to wing by wing
Has lost its symmetry. Marriages
Under the one roof are an upward
Curve. Children count from great-
Grandchildren in dozens, half-dozens,
Not twos or threes. Paint on wood
Go back to another age, one
Sewn up inside the pitch of a gas-lamp,
Signing arms and our voices map.

    Boundaries you had to respect,
    Fictions you now inspect.

So many layers has the wood spongy,
A feel you double-take every time.
To restore banisters and stairs,
You move through captured rainbows
Picking up sheer grain at last.
Brace yourself for the names;
Eraser, not restorer; rubbing out
Your own thumbprint and the dead's
Defenceless save your belief in ghosts.

    Boundaries you had to respect,
    Fictions you now inspect.

Later, you examine your thumbs,
Naked, you'd clothe them in those
Several layers against the years:
A first brushstroke steered by
Your guide's steady pressure,
Your hand in his, fleshy and warm.
A direction you learn, then resist,
Resisting until it lets you go,
To find a groove all yours.

    Boundaries you had to respect,
    Fictions you now inspect.

AIRY HALL'S FEATHERED GLORIES

Birds the ambitious among us trap.
We spend life hearing songs from this one,
Boasts from that; sticks, sticks, sticks,
At inviting angles, covered in gum
These bird-catchers chew till jaws ache,
Mixed with something bled from trees.

They hide, sights on the planted sticks;
We mill, one stork-foot against our lean;
All track as best they can a bird's pelt
Across the open: an impossible curve,
Dead stops in thin air, about turns,
Pirouettes, spinning our heads.

As a bird lands we see its changes.
From surprise anchored in stillness –
A stillness buoyed by such quiet,
A quiet of knowing what's what –
To wing-beats, loose feathers,
Cries that make us stop our ears,

Look away or clamp eyelids. Inside,
The last lighted image: a stick
Swaying with capture, fuelling,
Refuelling; a gum taste far back
On the upper palate and a song
Singled out from scores in an aviary.

After an absence hard to string
A sentence in, ambition itself,
Nursed from crawl, to walk, to run,
Enters the brashest of suns, cages
Held high as lamps, mirrors or trophies
Brimming a tongue-tied, granite dark.

AIRY HALL'S COMMON DENOMINATORS

The road's equatorial run
Through Airy Hall;
Houses, whitewashed or mud-daubed,
Blinded by trees that catch sand
Before the grains lodge in slatted windows;
A trench, parched or flooded,
Bleached or submarine,
According to one of two seasons.

Add a solitary donkey
Braying at midday the moment its harness
Lifts away for lunch; its short trot
And hind-legs-buck as it settles to graze;
A crow to peck puffed-up ticks
Rosy-mouthed and leathery.

Rice someone sat and picked clean
All morning on the veranda has swelled,
Full as the sifted flour is brown;
A stew gurgles and will hold its readiness
For the rest of the day if necessary —

It is hardly necessary;
You scrape your bare feet on the matting,
Push past the swinging half-doors
Hat in hand, blinking in the halved light.

AIRY HALL WARD

There will be days when you or I are bedridden,
Unable to stomach direct light or a voice.
Who fly-posts town?
Word spreads faster than the virus
Rusting the joints; weeks' worth of picked fruit
Turns the whole place into an orchard.

It's enough to make anyone get up.
All this loving and understanding
That's just there for when
You're in a bad way
And all the time I'm thinking
They must have the wrong address altogether:

The door-knocker that had to be silenced
With a bandage, the children shooed
From the sick part of the house –
Partitioned, horticulturally sound,
And a solid stillness
You had to whisper in and labour through.

AIRY HALL AUTUMN

A gust flips
the white undersides
of leaves
to the light.
Some loosen,
describe a slowed,
ziggurat fall.

We dash one way,
jab air another
to catch any.
Most grip a thick dark,
framing in mid-air
the four corners
of stars stared at.

For the feel
as their dry spines
crumble in your moist palm –
its kept warmth,
veined as a new leaf,
keeping all seasons –
grab, be airborne and grab.

AIRY HALL'S EXITS

Salt over the shoulder
Or a trip curtailed,
On account of the black cat
That crossed your path.

Last rites for the sick
In a house a crow
Overflew or preened itself on
And cawed, cawed, cawed.

A black dress, the gift
From a relative you've never seen,
For the funeral of a friend
You never imagined could die.

The dream you fall in,
Waking seconds before you land,
Your heart backfiring; the dream
You one day fail to wake from.

AIRY HALL'S DARK AGE

Someone's, 'The child is a cross,
He has bad blood through and through,'
Is picked up and amplified across fields.

These vocals stick somehow in the acres
This town covers, against a gale
On its way to tearing up islands.

A child doing the things
Children do: sly, brash, fidgety,
Becomes aligned with the devil.

All that remains is for one among us
To fetch the pint-sized stake
Dressed in razor-grass and bramble.

No sooner the child is ambushed,
An empty paddy bag he raced in
Swooped over his head and tied,

Rough-shod about waist level,
A lasso from a hand he looked up to
And he is beyond us all.

AIRY HALL RAIN

Fat, roomy, dust-raising drops,
Close ranks and wall up space:
Steady rain for days . . .

A lullaby, it sends us off early;
Or huddled, our voices low,
Up to our necks in bedding.

We hear of lost bridges,
Holes where a road should be,
A house on stilts turned ark.

Before the mustiness and absence,
Some of us will lose friends,
Wondering about insects and birds

That must hide and feed somewhere;
Forgetting the rain like a heart,
Pulsed and faltering when a beat misses.

AIRY HALL AT NIGHT

I

Moonlight cushions thought,
Rounds the hard edge of fence
Gate and tarpaulin, brings the pond
At the bottom of the yard
To the swinging half-doors
You duck through
As light wades into darknesses;
A counter-flap you lift
Turning 180° to face where you came,
Lowered with a strangled thud.

II

A night without stars, moon or lamplight,
Lowers heads in its tent;
Flaps drawn at the corners and pegged
To moistening ground. Accept
If you walk for long enough
You'd hit a wall that gives a little
Before gathering itself
To send you reeling back.
Now the insects' clatter makes sense,
It is time to leave.

III

If you step on a toad,
You will know you have stepped on a toad.
You cannot forget what you have done.
You wash your foot, towel it,
And still feel the trodden toad
Underfoot: how you jumped higher
Than any toad, using the toad's back
As a trampoline; how it worked as one,
Though sunk inches into dry earth
Bounding out of sight as if a finger

Had pushed it, head and body down,
Not a foot stepped on its back.
We see them ride each other for hours,
Motionless or dragging their bellies
Over fields to a secluded spot;
Fill their necks like trumpet players
And blast the night open; we see all this
Remembering the exact pressure of frogs
On our soles. We shake heads to clear them;
The frogs stick as if rooted there.

AIRY HALL ISOTOPE

Consider our man in a hovel
With no windows, a shack our missiles
Sail through; cracks that do not interrupt
The flow of moonlight or sunlight,
Seen here washing or baking his floor.

Consider too, our woman, reputed to fly
At night on the very broom that sweeps
Her yard printless; the same broom
Used to swipe Dog eyeing Hen's egg,
Noisily announced by Hen, drooled over
By Dog that is hungry, hungry;
Dreaming the one dream starring Hen.

Consider last, any boy convalescing
In a house crucified between those two
(How he was among the first to fling
Sand stones), spreadeagled
In her mud hut, she massages him
After two days in a pain she alone
Kills with her curious touch.

Consider these and you have a life,
Several lives lapping the one sun,
Casting the same lengthening shadows
From a moon so strapping, the children
Play bat and ball and make clean catches.

AIRY HALL NIGHTMARE

You sleep little and light
In a bed made for two big people.
Now the springs are brands;
Now electric rings;
Now nails stacked close as bristles.

You are in this bed on the open sea
Strapped under bedding tucked in tight,
Without the strength to lift your arm,
The one with a thousand needles
Or stripped of all nerves, it's not yours.

Nose down in a pillow,
How can you shift the boulder
That is your likeness,
Greying by the second?
With sheer will? How indeed.

AIRY HALL LEAVE-TAKING

Talk about leaving Airy Hall
Remains just that – talk.
Down to the last man to disappear
Round the bend from Airy Hall.

A town turned out to watch
His broad back rhythmically tot up
Almost obsolete yards between his past
And a future he erased with each blind step.

His name was a buzz, then a hum,
Then hardly a breath.
Now it is an absence,
The best of us could not fill.

His was the shadow of the man that left,
Found in a kennel owned by
The mangy dog he threw scraps at
When he was someone:

We forget his name; we think we hear
A man yelp where a dog should be;
Who can be sure at this late hour
Or ever.

THE COW *PERSEVERANCE*

I

Here I am writing you on old newspaper against a tide of
  print,
In the regular spaces between lines (there are no more trees).
I've turned it upside-down to widen the gap bordering sense
  and nonsense,
For what I must say might very well sound as if it were topsy
  turvy.
I put myself in your shoes (unable to recall when I last set eyes
  on a pair).
You read everything twice, then to be doubly sure, aloud,
Testing their soundness: *we wash cow's dung for its grain,*
And I feel your stomach turn; it's not much unlike collecting it
  for fuel,
Or mixed with clay to daub cracks in our shelters and renew
  door-mounds
That free us of rain, insects and spirits. They no longer drop
  the milk
We let them live for; their nights spent indoors for safe keep,
Their days tethered to a nearby post. People eye them so, they
  are fast becoming our cross.

II

Hunger has filled them with what I can only call compassion.
Such bulbous, watery eyes blame us for the lack of grass and
  worse,
Expect us to do something; tails that held the edge of
  windscreen wipers
In better days, swishing the merest irritant, a feather's even,
Let flies congregate until the stretched, pockmarked hide is
  them.
That's why, when you asked how things were, I didn't have to
  look far,
I thought, *Let the cow explain, its leathery tongue has run this
  geography
Many times over;* how milk turns, unseen, all at once, so lush
  pastures
Threw up savannahs. The storms are pure dust or deep inside
  the rowdiest
Among us, virtually dead and rowdy because they know it,
  they're not sure what else to do.

III

We watch its wait on meagre haunches, ruminating on what
  must be
Imperishable leather, some secret mantra, our dear buddha, for
  the miracle
We need; and us, with nowhere to turn, find we believe. God
  knows
It's a case of choosing which pot-hole in the road to ride;
  knowing
We export the asphalt that could fill them; knowing too the
  one thing
We make these days that is expressly ours is whipped in
  malarial water
And forced down our throats for daring to open our mouths.
Give us the cow's complicity any day: its perfect art of being
  left
In peace; its till-now effortless conversion of chewy grass to
  milk;
And its hoof-print, ignored for so long though clearly
  trespassing.
Then we too can jump over the moon, without bloodshed.
The cow's raised-head and craned-neck attempt
Is a tale you and I are bound to finish, in flesh or spirit.

ONLY THE PRESIDENT'S EGGS ARE YELLOW

Everyone else's resembles
Condensed milk; 'sunny-side up'
Offered as a snide alternative.

All desires boil down to a visa,
A queue, longer than the electorate,
Half the national football team
Jumped, disappearing on tour.

The electric grid scrimps at half-strength.
Videos wait, doubling as bases for plants;
Televisions reflect exactly what is around them;
Fridges like empty coffins have a wise patience,
Keeping stale air stale at sauna-temperature.

A hundred-year tree the country's new main road
Circumnavigated either side to pass,
Spontaneously uprooted; my first cousin
Planted a nimble offshoot in its place;
In a tropics where the rains are simply due,
Its youth showed, wilting in the heat.

This democracy is forced-ripe, for what?
You can tell by how newer and newer conscripts
Dismiss being dunked, feet-up in water-barrels;
How they carry themselves as if smelling
Responsibilities far above their stations;
How they dash grudging salutes at civilians
Earmarked for nursed rounds of ammunition

(Bursting with too much importance to notice).
The American Embassy tends all their street's
Litter and trees, painted in brilliant stockings;
Shutters angled to see out, not in;
A private generator to cook cold air and ice.
I had to crawl for a visa to enter the country;

Not because I'm an undesirable, it's unwritten
Policy in line with giant economies.
A clerk supplements a low salary anyhow;
Washing one shirt every night; without
Deodorants, a skunk an hour into the day.

A strapping man, about my age, with bare feet
Begged me for any loose change I could spare.
I emptied all the tinny noise in my pockets
Into his cupped hands: 'Thanks, English.'

By twelve o'clock egg and sun look alike:
Whole office blocks are warped L.P.s;
A gross tremor threatening the real.

EARTH

In the end we come to you prostrated.

We bear a black mark on our foreheads,
Once the Muezzin's preserve.

You open for our entry clean as a dive
Whose rings — a trunk's year's stockpile —
Are all the pool widens.

STONE AND SHELL

I used a stone to pound a shell;
I pounded it to smithereens,
Then ground it into dust.

Now the shell is hushed;
I weigh the stone against the dust.

A GREAT HOUSE BY THE SEA

The routine jab
becomes a form of torture.
A door held for someone
important, too long,
loses its perfumed environment
for one fumigated.

One man dies,
another steps into his shoes;
a mother's final cry
begins her child's.

This house is big enough
for us to stay lonely.
There are books to outlast life,
rooms for a small drama,
an invited audience,
and a scullery, marble table *in situ*.

Our first smell of the sea
is dead flesh we mistake
for poison;
this night air is shitty.
We race indoors for body odour,
for air fired by central heating.
Our voices carry so well
it takes forever to find ourselves.

I BURIED MY FATHER A COMPLETE STRANGER

One close day in E5 or E6, the mute hearse
rounded the corner and filled his street.

At the parlour I looked and looked
at the boy asleep. I could have kissed him
on his brow with every hair in place.

We stood by empty seats shifting our weight,
drove deliberately to a hole made for him,
buried the child and took the man away.

SPIRIT-LEVEL

I've not seen a sky like it since:
A heavy blue, except for a flame's fringe.

I searched it for the usual shapes
That shift from one known thing to another.

It gave nothing of itself save this blue,
Lightening; reddened at the heart

Of something. As a medical team waits
On the first aquamarine spike

From a wired cardiac arrest, so I braced
For this build-up, its every colourful trapping

Moulted to touch I'm not sure what.
Any sign of a quickening in me would do.

Thank goodness my life didn't depend on it.
There I was, stuck till a cramp set in,

Seeing chimneys begin their long exhalations
In that drifting place between roof and sky –

Passing too easily as cloud – and spires
Trained on some target exactly beyond.

As if I'd been asleep on my feet, a light
I couldn't look at direct made me jump:

Providing I steered clear of names
Gift-wrapped for me, it might always climb.

From *British Subjects*

GRANNY ON HER SINGER SEWING MACHINE

You think you are a bird and your station is the sky?
Lick the thread and feed it through the needle's eye.

Are you an eagle or a hawk prepared to kill and die?
Lick the thread and feed it through the needle's eye.

When the enemy clips your wings explain how you'll fly?
Lick the thread and feed it through the needle's eye.

You hardly smell your sweat, don't fall for the old lie;
Lick the thread and feed it through the needle's eye.

A GIFT OF A ROSE

Two policemen (I remember there were at least two)
stopped me and gave me a bunch of red, red roses.
I nursed them with ice and water mixed with soluble aspirin.
The roses had an instant bloom attracting stares
and children who pointed; toddlers cried and ran.

This is not the season for roses everyone said,
you must have done something to procure them.
I argued I was simply flashed down and the roses
liberally spread over my face and body to epithets
sworn by the police in praise of my black skin and mother.

Others told me to take care of the flowers, photo them,
a rare species, an example for others, a statistic;
that the policemen should be made a return gift
crossed several minds – a rose for a rose.
With neglect, they shrivelled and disappeared,

people stopped looking when I went Saturday-shopping.
Though I was deflowered, a rose memory burned clear.
Now when I see the police ahead, I take the first exit;
I even fancy I have a bouquet of my own for them;
I pray they'll keep their unseasonable gifts to themselves.

HOME

These days whenever I stay away too long,
anything I happen to clap eyes on,
(that red telephone box) somehow makes me
miss here more than anything I can name.

My heart performs a jazzy drum solo
when the crow's feet on the 747
scrape down at Heathrow, H.M. Customs . . .
I resign to the usual inquisition,

telling me with Surrey loam caked
on the tongue, home is always elsewhere.
I take it like an English middleweight
with a questionable chin, knowing

my passport photo's too open-faced,
haircut wrong (an afro) for the decade;
the stamp, British Citizen, not bold enough
for my liking and too much for theirs.

The cockney cab driver begins chirpily
but can't or won't steer clear of race,
so rounds on Asians. I lock eyes with him
in the rearview when I say I live with one.

He settles at the wheel grudgingly,
in a huffed silence. Cha! Drive man!
I have legal tender burning in my pocket
to move on, like a cross in Transylvania.

At my front door, why doesn't the lock
recognize me and budge? I give an extra
twist and fall forward over the threshold
piled with the felicitations of junk mail,

into a cool reception in the hall.
Grey light and close skies I love you.
Chokey streets, roundabouts and streetlamps
with tyres chucked round them, I love you.

Police officer, your boots need re-heeling.
Robin Redbreast, special request — a burst
of song so the worm can wind to the surface.
We must all sing for our suppers or else.

AT THE GRAVE OF THE UNKNOWN AFRICAN

I

Two round, cocoa faces, carved on whitewashed headstone,
protect your grave against hellfire and brimstone.

Those cherubs with puffed cheeks, as if chewing gum,
signal how you got here and where you came from.

More than two and a half centuries after your death,
the barefaced fact that you're unnamed feels like defeat.

I got here via Whiteladies Road and Black Boy Hill,
clues lost in these lopsided stones that Henbury's vandal

helps to the ground and Henbury's conservationist
tries to rectify, cleaning the vandal's pissy love nest.

African slave without a name, I'd call this home
by now. Would you? Your unknown soldier's tomb

stands for shipload after shipload that docked,
unloaded, watered, scrubbed, exercised and restocked

thousands more souls for sale in Bristol's port;
cab drivers speak of it all with yesterday's hurt.

The good conservationist calls it her three hundred year war;
those raids, deals, deceit and capture (a sore still raw).

St Paul's, Toxteth, Brixton, Tiger Bay and Handsworth;
petrol bombs flower in the middle of roads, a sudden growth

at the feet of police lines longer than any cricket pitch.
African slave, your namelessness is the wick and petrol mix.

Each generation catches the one fever love can't appease;
nor Molotov cocktails, nor when they embrace in peace

far from that three-named, two-bit vandal and conservationist
binning beer cans, condoms and headstones in big puzzle pieces.

II
Stop there black Englishman before you tell a bigger lie.
You mean me well by what you say but I can't stand idly by.

The vandal who keeps coming and does what he calls fucks
on the cool gravestones, also pillages and wrecks.

If he knew not so much my name but what happened to Africans,
he'd maybe put in an hour or two collecting his Heinekens;

like the good old conservationist, who's earned her column
inch, who you knock, who I love without knowing her name.

The dead can't write, nor can we sing (nor can most living).
Our ears (if you can call them ears) make no good listening.

Say what happened to me and countless like me, all anon.
Say it urgently. Mean times may bring back the water cannon.

I died young, but to age as a slave would have been worse.
What can you call me? Mohammed. Homer. Hannibal. Jesus.

Would it be too much to have them all? What are couples up
to when one reclines on the stones and is ridden by the other?

Will our talk excite the vandal? He woz ere, like you are now,
armed with a knife, I could see trouble on his creased brow,

love-trouble, not for some girl but for this village.
I share his love and would have let him spoil my image,

if it wasn't for his blade in the shadow of the church wall
taking me back to my capture and long sail to Bristol,

then my sale on Black Boy Hill and disease ending my days:
I sent a rumble up to his sole; he scooted, shocked and dazed.

Here the sentence is the wait and the weight is the sentence.
I've had enough of a parish where the congregation can't sing.

Take me where the hymns sound like a fountain-washed canary,
and the beer-swilling, condom-wielding vandal of Henbury,

reclines on the stones and the conservationist mounts him,
and in my crumbly ears there's only the sound of them sinning.

DOMESTIC FLIGHT

I heard what I took for wind chimes
3000 feet above London's lights,
each light a small sound.

The pearl necklaces of traffic
break, trying to get round
my neck of the woods.

The Thames ribbed and corseted
by traffic despite its peregrinations
in a black wetsuit.

Occasionally real diamonds startle
at high points in the city.
Gold is on the horizon, a rim.

Some distance below us an insect
with a compound look and rotating wings
hightails it home with bare ski feet.

The river is Sanskrit in black ink
scribbling away into the dark,
turning over with each tide.

From *Bill of Rights*

Goodbye Chattanooga. Hello Potaro.
Later, L— and Brixton. Essequibo, here we go.

Someone they call a buck light-footed
It over to me. I jumped but his open palms,

A stupid smile and his near-naked frame
Put me at ease. He gave me corn

I bolted down. His head shake, finger wag
And suppressed chuckle told me I'd done wrong.

This is not a portion of potato
Chips wrapped in salt and vinegar – what a hog! –

Wrapped in turn in yesterday's news, that suited
Me fine for supper, that went down a charm

Chased with a can of shandy and a shame-
-less belch close to speech, full of scorn

For having to chew each mouthful sixteen gawd
Awful times, virtually digesting it on the tongue.

Dip the tip of an arrow in this plant sap,
Let it dry, untouched, in the sun,
Let it fly into that wild boar.

Roast the boar but offer some to the sun,
Carve buttons from the bone,
Dry the skin, tell the boar you are sorry

But you have a thousand mouths to feed
And it fits the bill exactamundo.

Add to these plant sap
Taste of a tangerine sun
Wild in the meat of that boar
Roast from that aluminium sun
Buttons in those bones
Eyes in those buttons you tell sorry
Thousand mouths you have to feed
A thousand grins feeding you
Bill that boar fits exactly

Bow tie, bodacious, Father. Model divine Daddy.
Friend of Lenin. Friend of Amin. Friend of Stalin.
Here the Trades rinse the air constantly.
Rain returns the verdant to grass, trees and paling.

'All the days of my life, ever since I been born
I never heard a man speak like this man before.'
1000 Tarzan yodels tear the night to ribbons.

Night flutters in the breeze in shreds
Cries strike the dark with the spark of fireflies
To wave a mosquito from the forehead
Takes more effort than to clear this forest
Clear this continent of all of its wood
Burn that wood into smoke into cloud
Spread that cloud over the entire planet
Sink our planet into a black hole
Send that hole spinning into unknown space

Holy is coconut with cream and water
Holy stinking-toe and sour-sop and eddoe
Holy this vision in Him that brought us here
Holy His name Jones and His every aspect

Holy am I for my proximity to Him
Holy this Uzi blessed in service to Him
Holy every drop that rains and rusts our joints
Holy the hard wood greenheart in these huts.

Holy Him holy me holy you
Holy this holy that holy de-tarat!
Holy the serpent of temptation
Holy Pontius Pilate holy Judas Iscariot

Holy this sun uncut through rain
Holy the Buckoo Jumby Ol' Higue
Holy that giant pearl elasticated on water
Holy water gyrating underneath that weightless jewel

Autochthonous wood.
Purpleheart and greenheart
Blunted or broke electric
Saw after electric saw

In half. Wood this tough
Cannot have known much love
And must have hardened itself
Against further loss of face.

Against further time loss
Against further body loss
Against further mind loss
Against further soul loss
Against further blood loss
Against further life loss
Against further loss

In Chattanooga as in Kalamazoo
We had three square meals, inside loos
And an inside to speak of.

Here in paradise, Essequibo, Potaro,
The branch's leak never switches off.
I have the runs and chigoe,

A fungus culture between my toes.
I patrol this new town's perimeter
With my finger on an Uzi's trigger.

Rain our metronome
Rain our gait
Rain our habits
Rain our wake-up call
Rain our lullaby
Rain our flotilla
Rain our love
Rain our life
Rain our whore
Rain heaven
Rain hell
Rain God
Rain Devil

Yoknapatawpha county,
This was not.

Rice for breakfast,
Rice water soup for lunch –
Yes there was time for lunch –
Rice and beans for dinner,

With the stubborn giant anteater,
The sloth and the caiman,
Too tough by far,
Even for our meagre pots.

In this dream
There's no word for rice
No picture for rice
No taste for rice
No smell for rice
No touch no sound
No imagining rice

Topsoil gone in the rain with our seedlings.
Spirit for fighting back this wilderness gone
Too; all that's left unencumbered is my love
For Father: my nerves are a Stradivarius

In the hands of a musical pygmy.
Inside I sound like cats in an alley
Mating or squabbling over a smell of fish.
My face is as expressionless as a satellite dish.

Fingertips gone
Thumbprint too
Heels bone sore
Toes stiff stumps
Palms raw
Instep raw
Knees can't bend
Not even for God
Nor land nor flag
Not even for Father

Flint flicked into flames.
Two sticks, greenheart or purpleheart,
Rubbed together until they catch.

Our matches are moist and useless.
Kerosene wicks drown in the mist.
The vines are flame-shaped,

Cold and green as moss. Leaves leap,
Curl, crawl as if out of control.
Their razored edges cut and burn.

Razor grass moon
Flint stick sun
Needling rain
Obeah moon
Witching sun
Stone rain
Laser sun

Brixton market was rough but this is rougher.
I could find saltfish and eddoes near the reggae
Shop that shook my fillings and made my ears ring.

A 37 bus always came eventually –
Often after a long wait – in twos and threes.
And at my council flat there was a hook

Behind the door and a jabbering set
That snowed, drizzled, then cleared after a thump.

Chump chump went the piranhas
On the children who jumped
Unthinkingly into the river
During a spell without supervision
Oh red river
Howls under water
Blood signalling miles downstream
For more, more piranhas to come feast

The Front Line can be scary
But the banks of the Potaro are scarier.

I used gum on a stick to capture a canary,
Locked it in a bamboo cage and waited for its aria.

But it stayed dumb and I grew hungrier
And hungrier, caring less for its song

And more for its meat, and succumbed
Losing most of the meagre roast to the griot.

A man pulled a knife on me for stepping on his alligator shoes
Another saw me ask for change on a street corner and thought
I was moving in on his turf to push weed of my own

The only weed I know pushes through concrete fourteen storeys
Up the sides of my council flat tower block
Come sun rain gale sleet or snow

What a feisty griot! He talked with his mouth
Full and told his story in instalments,
Silenced by morsels of that canary.

I went without for a story full of the warm South.
That griot didn't even leave me bones.
He chewed them to powder;

Except for one bone which he hollowed
Into a flute and played and lulled me to sleep.

What canary bone?
Human more like!
Weren't we fine young cannibals?
Seeing a canary as we munched
Instead of you or me
Made swallowing easier
Or else the jaws would have clamped
Down seized-up locked shop jammed shut

Not a dreamless sleep, one with nightmares.

Men, women and children queue before a pot
More like a vat and drink or else are shot,

Their cries that could raise the dead, raise hair
And a thousand flutes in a death air,

A thousand flutes piled on top
Each other, like so many grains of rice.

Trained on a meandering line of souls
From Brixton, Chattanooga and Kalamazoo,

Was an Uzi, I knew, held the way I do.

A thousand flutes for bullets
A thousand souls for flutes
A thousand bullets for souls

I woke with Cassandra Wilson's Tupelo
Honey on my mind and a snapshot –
Me guarding our reverend leader's pot
Of plenty with my finger on my trusted Uzi.

Drink, I was ordering them, Drink,
As I tapped out that tune on the trigger
When my head cleared it was the reverse –
One of those Kodak Instamatics and silence.

Silence except for the baying of the blood
Silence above the wind in the trees
Silence as the river breaches its banks
Silence of us like fish in a tank
Silence in the lengthening plait of vines
Silence so that Father can catch forty winks

Nails driven home with rubber hammers
Teeth flying from a bandaged fist
A headlock until somebody or other goes limp
Hands over the mouth and nose until some face blues
All ship-shape while Father gets his shut-eye

From planting on a hillside
Under an unsheltering sky
To banana leaves for a roof
To these shingled wood huts

Took time, but we had help
From a government, tribes,
And God like a man in our midst
Telling what came to pass.

What came to pass
Has come to pass
Has come and gone
Came and went

What came to pass
That has not always passed
Already came and passed
What comes must pass

What came to pass
Came and did not pass
Did come did pass
Had come had passed

What came to pass
Came to stay with us
Came in fact for us
Came and we passed

There is a relevant passage in the Good Book
For this season of pestilential rain
For our crops that refuse to grip hills

For the mosquito that sings as it sucks us dry
For watersnakes, manatees and marabuntas
For the hours when we huddle for warmth

For nothing no thing catches to make fire
For our God who preaches patience
Who by example starves and falls into a fit

That relevant passage slips my mind
Slips from the Good Book
From this rain forest
This wet world
From this moment referred to as
That slippery passage
That irrelevant passage
That not-so-good Book
That so-so Book
That kiss-me-arse Book
That rain rain that never fucks off
That world beyond this arse-hole forest

[. . .]

Bearded vines clutch at ankles,
Hands and heads. Streets here are wind-
Made or water-travelled; not for foot.

Our feet are winged by our faith.
We rip those vines from their roots
Even as they rip our flesh off our bones.

We feel our faith bolster with each test
So feel nothing: doubts are the worms
We pull for each other from our flesh.

Pull and eat
Pull and cry
Pull and lay down and die
Pull and multiply
Pull and try not to break
Pull and faint
Pull and pull
Till we can't pull anymore

I was there
When Jones cracked
His one and only joke

He called Guyana's
Bracken-tumbling
Savannahs

Blasted
Flat-arsed
Country

Such exaggerated
Ceaseless laughter
As there was

The likes of which
Had never been heard
Before or since

In those jungle
Confines curbed
Only when Jones

Failing
With his hand
Held high

And repeated
Dismissive waves
Suddenly

Lost his temper
Pulled off his belt
And beat everyone

Within reach
Ignoring his trousers
Around his feet

I can testify
The man never wore
Any skids

Or underpants
Swing low
Sweet chariot

Father, this well too deep.
This well too dark, Father.
Big hands and feet, push me
Under water, Father.

Give me your purpleheart
Or greenheart stave to this
Father; a stinging lash
That when it's over, it's

Over; but I carry
This water for days, Father,
After that night, that well
Never leaves me, Father.

Water in the well
Till the well run dry
Is not the truth I a-tell
Is pure lie
Lie pure like water
I a-tell

If the R's could see their daughter
Now. A lady in waiting. She hath drunk
Honeydew for too long and tasted ... not!

Coffee's ghost lingers among the vines
And that snake doubling as a bird is Quetzal-
coatl, in those vines swinging from tree

To misted tree, vines my cutlass
Bounces off. Lay lady lay.

Daughter of the revolution
Daughter of the dust
Daughter of the water course
Daughter without a past
Daughter born big so
Daughter born voluptuous so
Daughter born wise so
Speak to us

[...]

Savannah, raced by bundles of bracken,
Raced by the uninterrupted wind,
Raced, in turn, by someone, equal in stature
To the Reverend.

God is in His heaven.
The People's Temple know Him as a statue
That comes to life with the wave of a wand
In the form of our Jim, that can't be broken.

As the savannah races towards the forest
The forest retreats towards the river

As the river reaches for us
We plant with our backs to the trees

The savannah knows God watches
The forest knows it too

Yet the savannah advances
Still the forest beats its retreat

Someone's wife, she was Waiyaki or Makusi.
She said she washed her waist-length hair
On the stony banks of the Mazaruni.

I doubted her; not. She thought I resembled
One of C.L.R.'s Black Jacobins. I trembled
With unadulterated lust, not for her,

But for handfuls of her hair and the rest
Under us like an eiderdown in our love-nest.

Someone's wife is always sweeter
Makes you want to grab and eat her
Standing sitting lying down
Frontwards backwards round and round

Someone's wife is someone's traitor
Another's boss secretary neighbour
Standing sitting lying down
Frontwards backwards round and round

[. . .]

Stabroek market has a broken clock.
The time it tells is always right

Twice, then there is the time it doesn't tell.
Like how long this country can go without

Flour, rice, sugar, potato, corn,
Soap, oil, and anything else you care to list.

For as long as that clock can tell the time
And this whole market of shoppers not give a damn.

Back to back
In the face of adversity

Belly to belly
Rub your love all over me

We don't give a damn
This country dying slowly

I done dead already
Don't bother bury me

[. . .]

If a man acquired a cart, without a horse,
To sell mauby, shaved ice, coconut water,

By walking Georgetown, would it be a case
Of out the frying pan into the fire,

On account of Georgetown's choke and robbers
Lethal as coral snakes? A man could do worse

Than roam the capital blowing his own trumpet,
Like stay here and end up in a hearse.

But that would put Descartes before the Hobbes
We know and love; and that would put an end to verse.

Cart horse
Horse ice
Ice water
Water fire
Fire choke
Choke robber
Robber snake
Snake coral
Coral man
Man city
City love
Love verse
Verse hearse
Hearse trumpet
Trumpet love
Love cart
Cart love
Love fire
Fire love
Love water
Water love
Love love

Flood. Crops wasted away again.
Sun is a sign from far above.
We are ready to eat grubs
And the bark of trees,

When this army truck
Laden with tins and bread
Pulls into our compound –
A thank-you note from the President.

Make it funky – da dada dada da da
Make it funky
Provisions from the provider
President who has put the y
Back in our funk

Make it funky – da dada dada da da
Make it funky – domdom dom domdom
Funky President-e Yeah!

Thank my Uzi give me some ammo.
And some grease – Uzi food.
I have learned to tell the time by the sun

When I can see it in a clearing
Or free of cloud and by the way light
Lifts a long flowing skirt and crosses

The paddy field and the paddy bows
In suppliance. Light is greater than our Reverend.

Light hoods our eyes
Light creases our foreheads
Light makes our bones porous
Light darkens our skin
Light peels our heads
Light lifts us off the ground
Light puts us underground
Light forks our tongues
Light loosens teeth in our gums
Light tightens clitoris and scrotum

I tap the acacia tree for gum,
The coconut for milk,
The palm tree for wine.

I feel like that tapster Tutuola
Bumped off on page one, except
None have come or will ever tackle

This jungle to find me, so I tap, tap, tap,
Like Woody Woodpecker, minus the cackle,
While another drinks, drinks, drinks.

Woodpecker with one shoe
Tap tap tapping
On the windowless wood
A spider couldn't sound better
Morse none can decipher
Tell me the formula
For wine for milk for gum

If not a formula a recipe will do
If not a recipe
Say hello to my Uzi
In any language you please
I'll use your colourful quiff
As a puffed up cravat
And your beak for that unreachable itch

I eat from a leaf called the dasheen
My fingers are my knife and fork
I use grass to wipe my ass
Bathe beneath the clear cannon

Of a waterfall

Breeze towels my skin then a jolt
Wakes me from the one dream and I go
Work in the fields or tapping with a growl
In my belly and my belly on my mind.

My brains in my belly
My soul in my belly
My heart in my belly
My baby in my belly
My desire in my belly
My Muse in my belly
My God in my belly
My sins in my belly
My hopes in my belly
My dreams in my belly
My mother in my belly
My father in my belly
My wife in my belly
My children in my belly
My belly in my belly

The government truck that brings supplies
Is long overdue. Our leader got on the CB
And barked at some poor soul in Samson's
Office who wouldn't put Samson on the line.

Our leader threatened the wrath of God
Unless it rained bread, milk and wine
From the capital. Nunchakas, rice
Flails, greenheart clubs and my Uzi.

All the clouds are rice fields
Ready for harvest
All the clouds are coconut groves
Ripe for picking
All the clouds are sweet potatoes
Bubbling just below ground
All the clouds are a thousand plates
Brimming at an endless banquet
All the clouds are rolling by
Taking their promises elsewhere

Our leader likened our resolve to greenheart.
If this wood, he said, finger-wagging, wide-eyed,
Can find its way to London to buffer
Banks along the Thames, all the way – lover? –

From this interior we can surely establish
A toe-hold on the outskirts – under the skirts –
Or my name is not Jim Jones and we are not
The renowned People's Temple – we are not.

Blouse and skirts! Bumba cloth!
Rass cloth! Blood cloth!

Take the place of prayer
Our lexicon contracts to a hool

In a spool empty of cotton
A curse is as good as a song

Plate cloth! Kiss me rass!
Kiss me ass! Kiss me backside!

She is still with him or he with her.
She drinks directly from the fountain
Instead of from the trough. I miss her.

Her look says, you killed my husband
And brought me to this, therefore,
Sonny, you have zero hold over me.

She sits on her Mr Sheen hair beside him.
Love, there were others, will be others.

My love is true
Only as true
As I'm to you
As you're to me
As we're to us
And to ourselves
What is this love
What is this trust
What is this fuss
Without this love
Without this trust
Without this fuss
There is no me
There is no you
There is no us
Only a shell
An empty shell
An empty well
A silent drum
From here from now
From me to you
Till kingdom come
A measly crumb
Of what we are
Or could have been

No hosannas
Just bad manners
In bandannas
No myrrh
No manna
No frankincense
And all this life
A heavy load
A long sentence

There is a crop that can be grown in these hills
That won't wash away in the rain, that certain
Termites can't stomach, that fetches
A market price ten times that of rice.

Goodbye paddy field, good riddance sugar
Cane. Are we turning to good old bauxite?
No. Will it be prospecting for diamonds
Deeper in this quagmire like a pork-knocker?

When will we be delivered?
Answer
How long in this quagmire?
Answer
Why must the children suffer?
Answer
Where will we go from here?
Answer
What can you promise us now?
Answer
Will we still follow you?
Answer

No. This crop goes by several names:
Ganja, sinsimilla, marijuana, kaya,
Herb, ital, spliff, joint, fix, kale,
Spiritual food, the body of Christ,
The way to transubstantiation,
A means of escape from the shit-stem,
Food of the gods, opiate of the people;
Plant a seed, there is no sheriff to shoot.

You ask a man to watch the thing
He most craves
Watch but don't touch
Look but don't partake
Smell but don't taste
Imagine all he likes
But one false move . . .

[. . .]

Take me to one of those English shires,
Douse me in petrol and set me ablaze.
I'd swap all this Mittelholzer
For just one Morning At The Office.

I had no mother to call a father,
No palace nor chalice, nor spliff,
No dreads to shake at despotic authority;
Just me, my unrequited love for her
With the hair and my trusted, rusty Uzi.

When poetry dies my love for you dies too
Or put another way my love for you
Can never die not as long as there's
Breath in me not as long as there's
Poetry for me to breathe my love

In order for my love for you to die
Not only must I be dead but so must you
And not only us two but verse too
And how can verse be dead when all
There is to say about our love has not been said

Has hardly begun to be said in fact
I take it back poetry is everlasting
Which is to say it exists outside of time
In turn our love as a poem outstrips time
And once time is given the slip there's no dying

There's only the life of the love to live
In this case us versus timelessness
Us two sharing this love that won't die
Even as we blink in our lives and expire
Our lives no longer than a blink in time

Our love no less than time no more
Than life itself us in that love
With nothing to lose if we lose our lives
Since that love has slipped from time
From death and lives as life itself

I try hard to think outside the scripture,
And to hear, when I think, a voice other than
Our illustrious leader's.

For a long time I walked around in a blank
And could do nothing else but stand quite still
When I tried to conjure

An image of a boa constrictor; a tiger
Tiger burning bright; a long-legged fly
But grossed *nada*.

Tiger come to warm up the party
Tiger here to jive in the dancehall
Tiger going to put the tickle back in you
Tiger bring the spice to put in your stew

Everybody want to be a tiger
Everybody afraid of the tiger
Everybody says he's friends with tiger
Everybody good to eat to the tiger

Don't cuddle a boa constrictor
Don't put your head in tiger's mouth
Don't wrestle with an alligator
Even if you have faith procure doubt

[. . .]

If I had wings of a dove I would fly –
Where? Back to Brixton? Chattanooga?
Kalamazoo? I would settle for a nest
Comprised entirely of her Rapunzel plait.

But she lets it down for another,
And lies back on it like a mat,
And he wraps himself in what's
Left over and not a stitch between them;
And not a split end to spare me.

If love were a diet I'd be anorexic
for you
Thin as smoke on a blade of grass
for you
Light as a moonbeam on the iris
for you
Faint as a Dogstar at midday
for you
Dry-mouthed as a pothole in the Sahara
for you
Frond-lipped bruise-lipped puckered-lipped
for you
Static-skinned hangnail-ridden nose bleeding
for you
Wire my jaws warm water through straws
for you
Stone strapped to flatten my noisy belly
for you
Walkabout the four deserts of the Outback
for you
Nil by mouth nil by eyes nil by ears
for you
Rag and bone skin and bone bag of bones
for you

Less and less more or less less of me
for you

[. . .]

If that doesn't stir his precious gonads

He's dead down there or else this

Hasn't got to him because the postage

Fell short or a kleptomaniac

For a postman has put my penned gem

In a pile in his spare room filed under

Fantasy or magical realism

Brewed from the heart of the hops of the South
Poured from a glass in a pub in the mouth

Rinsed from an ass in a room with a view
Gulped in the throat through a wall in a loo

Rolled off the wrist of a friend for a laugh
Stored in a tube just in case he got gassed

Stuck in the face of a nun on the run
Spread on the breast of a girl just for fun

Licked off the bum off the face off the chest
Left there to dry and to peel and to crust

Brewed in the balls of the crotch of a man
Poured from the cock in the cunt of woman

Poured in the ass in the mouth in the hand
Poured on the flesh on the hair on the land

[. . .]

We had the notion that we'd walk
From Land's End to John o'Groats
Collecting signatures for a Bill
Of Rights, in our black and blue
Yachtings; collect enough names
To lay from one end of that land
To the other; then and only then
We'd hang up those shoes, what's
Left of them; that or never sing
Marley, Burning Spear, Tapazukie
As long as we drew English air . . .

Over a banana-skin climate
Over an orange-peel land
Over a blood-orange history
Over a star-apple kingdom
Over a pear-shaped people
Over a kiwi-fruit territory
Over a coconut-husk accent
Over a Granny-Smith culture
Over green-turnip weather
Over a courgette drama
Over an aubergine theatre
Over the potato moors
Over a split-pea valley
Over a channa wall
Over a grits seawall
Over a black-eyed pea sea
Over a sago moon
Over a penny-farthing lake
Over a runner-bean stream
Over banger-and-mash hills
Over a saveloy-and-chips Midlands
Over a vinegar rain
Over a blow-torch sun
Over a ketchup sun

Over a stethoscope wind
Over a sewer wind
Over a telescoped Island
Over a microscope Island
Over a shrink-wrapped Island
Over a gob-smacked Island
Over an I.O.U. nothing Island

[. . .]

Tikka becomes a mother, at 2.45 a.m.
I hear her curse the Reverend
As the midwife urges her to push.

Silence builds this edifice, crammed
Into the longest while, that a cry demolishes;
Then laughter through tears; then the Reverend

Curses my name, storms out and finds me,
Wrestles my Uzi from me, aims,
Fires once, twice, but it's jammed.

Clickety clack
Clippety clop
Hoppety hop
Stoppety stop
Droppety drop
Smackety smack
Slappety slap
Kickety kick
Stoppety stop
Droppety drop
Flippety flop
Fuckety fuck
Moppety mop
Punchety punch
Spittety spit
Grabbety grab
Stoppety stop
Droppety drop
Bloodety blood
Bleedety bleed
Droppety drop
Stoppety stop

'Get out and take her with you
And the damned baby.
If I lay eyes on you again boy
These hands will kill you.'

'Father, the child may be her husband's.
I lay with her one time on the banks
Of the Mazaruni, just the once.
Her husband must look a lot like me.'

Don't argue with Father
Argue with the weather
Don't argue with Father
Argue with the savannah
Don't argue with Father
Argue with the forest
Don't argue with Father
Argue with the river
Don't argue with Father
Argue with alligators
Don't argue with Father
Argue with yellow fever
Don't argue with Father
Argue with coral snakes
Choke and robbers piranahs
Poisoned arrows scorpions
But don't argue with Father

[. . .]

I was bleeding from my eyes
Some thing supplied to my tearducts
By my ineluctable gall bladder.

Hadn't it been removed at King's
Or Guy's? The stones put in a jar
So that when I opened my eyes in recovery

The first thing I clapped eyes on
Wasn't my sweetheart or even L—,
But them, staring back, admonishingly.

Rain through sun and I hear Father
Cut grass smell and I hear Father
Axe splitting wood and I hear Father
Sugar cane in my mouth and I hear Father
Ripe guava smell and I hear Father
Dry husk torn from coconut shell — Father

Donkey bray at midday and I hear Father
Dissipating jet trail and I hear Father
Ankle clutch of a vine and I hear Father
Dry eye baby cry and I hear Father
Mist in the trees and I hear Father
High tide grinding down stones — Father

Tamarind on my tongue and I hear Father
Gall in my mouth and I hear Father
Chest burn heart burn and I hear Father
Air too thick for lungs and I hear Father
Bone brittle bone sore and I hear Father
Big man bawl big woman pull hair — Father

Could I have two gall bladders?
There's one for the books.

Shadows cast from those crows strengthen.
Does that mean they're lower?

Or has the sun intensified?
Nothing's between sun and me but crows.

If they would be still for a moment,
I could pretend they were clouds.

Shame is the sweat on the back of the neck
Shame is the hair stood on end on a neck
Shame is the key on a string round the neck
Shame is the knot of a noose round the neck
Shame is the wrung and then strung up high neck
Shame is a pulse under skin round the neck
Shame is the cut artery in the neck
Shame is a bruise or a bite on the neck
Shame is a hole for a tube down the neck
Shame is a head that's too big for a neck
Shame is a head that's too small for a neck
Shame is the skin that's too loose on the neck
Shame is the strain looks like strings on the neck
Shame is a lump in the throat and the neck
Shame is the ring piled on ring round a neck
Shame is the shame of the shame of the neck

The lump under my pillow
Is my Uzi.

The lump in my breast pocket
Over my heart
Is my comatose watch.

The lump in my throat
That I can't swallow
Away, no matter how hard
I try, is what?

Strain into string
Ring piled on ring
Knot of a noose
Skin that's too loose
Lump in the throat
Neck of a stoat

[. . .]

But I do wake, on every occasion,
With my fever as my only companion.

And now this carrion and these crows.
And now their strengthening shadows.

Not sure which of the two suns
I feel warming my brittle bones

Is which. The fever low in the sky,
Or the fever inside my marrow.

Damn sure I don't care for either.

[. . .]

I left my village
And my village girl
For a town my age
Which is no age at all

I am stirring pepper
In a pepper pot
Memories for casrep
Memories for stock

[. . .]

Bubble, bubble, toil and trouble
Father, never any good at Scrabble,
Turned to the Bible
Then away from the Bible
Into Scriptures scripted by himself.

Scriptures scripted by the gifted
Is one thing, in the hands of the mediocre
And the wicked, it's slimy as okra,
a.k.a. Lady's Fingers (confused with bora).

'Make my funk the P-funk.'
He hummed as he stirred the vat
Full of uncarbonated, reconstituted
Kool-Aid, laced with cyanide.

It was the ganja singing, not him.
He'd earlier rolled something more akin
To a spring roll, it was so neat and fat,
Than a joint, and kept it all to himself.

Who dubbed the deadly concoction
Corentyne Thunder cocktail?
A liquid bullet? But told
The unsuspecting children
Daddy-Kool, and the old, elixir
To the gateway of heaven?

Who would have the honour
To blow out Father's ingenious
Brains first, then his paltry
Own almost immediately afterwards?

We tossed for it. I called. I lost.
That coin had heads on both sides.
Just as the flat sides of a cutlass
Stung all the same whichever side
Father used to slap our behinds.

We had to say thank you every time,
And smile, as for a camera
About to take the best aspect
Of ourselves, about to save our souls
For posterity, say cheese.

[. . .]

New Poems

AN OUT-EY

When my umbilical cord,
the mere stub of it
withered and fell away,
my parents buried it
in a garden in South East
London and promptly packed
me off to Guyana. I have
what they call an out-ey,
not much of one. It's fifteen
minutes of fame and mine,
happened a stone's throw
from the East Demerara river
when the girl next door wet
a Johnson's cotton bud
between her teeth and daubed
her cool, slick spittle on me.
She said short of methylated
spirits I would have to make
do with her spit and how
she could not countenance
a boy with a bunged up navel.
I smiled and shook my head
dismissively and tried to stop
my belly from wobbling
like the bowl of Jell-O
(I had earlier spooned into her
mouth topped with Carnation)
a Pyrex dish's shapely green
translucence left to form
on the top shelf of the fridge,
pudding that my mother
accused me of eating
with no regard for her and my
six brothers. She sent me
to bed without supper. All night
my stomach growled and kept me

twisting and turning awake.
I had to feel for my navel
to be sure it was not missing,
not gone with the girl sent
back to England by her parents
to within spitting distance –
so I fancied for months –
of the garden I cannot, in
all these years, seem to find.

AUTOBIOGRAPHY OF A STONE

I lay for a millennium in a bed of ice
until gravity dropped its sideways hammer
and opened a river in my bed.
The current wore me down –
its one-way traffic.
I crouched and became set in my ways.

The river drained and dredged and dried.
Next thing I was broken into two by a complete
stranger who wanted my heart, its bright stone
for his lover. He discarded my two halves
on a mountain of such pieces
until a child's hand shaped me in it,

one piece of me in each hand,
then united into a right side pocket
in a warm dark next to his thigh.
Next in a clear jar someone took trouble
soaking the label off, propped on a mantle above
a fireplace where I saw midnight love and its loss.

I could smell the lake and town reservoir
before he took me up, first my left side,
and leaned a little to his left and fired me
from the sling of his broad shoulder.
I skipped on the surface of that wrinkled lake
as if I fully intended to walk to the other side.

I wanted to reach the exact middle, that part
where water roots deepest and most still.
I heard him whoop and holler the number of skips.
I settled and waited for the rest of me.
He loaded me and fired again and counted
and exclaimed at the exact same number

as before: my walk on my toes,
the ballerina in me, me in my element,
my sign, my big bang in reverse, more air
than stone in those moments
on that dimpled face whose cold
rubbed me up the wrong way.

I fell together almost as neatly
as I had broken apart. All I needed now
was my stolen heart. I prayed for
that lover who owned it to find her way
to this lake, row out to its still centre,
drown over me.

BEAVER

asleep improbably, in the road,
burst bundle, dribbling red untidily,
I am approaching you, wake up,
run and hide in the perennial shrub,
wait crouched, as bush the colour
your thick coat takes on, trembles,
until this bulk on two legs that is me
straying far from myself, trundles past,
then go back and snuggle down
in your unmade bed of the dead.

FOOT PRINT
(for baby Christopher)

If cartilage, muscle, nail and gristle
fill a shot-glass, and the little
that's a lot pours tidily into a pouch
no bigger than a sparrow's throat,
then your foot, delicate as a thistle,
eight months old and frost-brittle,
occupies exactly this open mouth
leather shoe, light enough to float.

Son, mould yourself to your first pair
for the heady climb from knees and hands.
Once up and running, what you wear,
not your soles, scorches in hot sands,
wards off corns, bunions, claw toes:
shoes fit for feet, feet fit for shoes.

JASPER, TEXAS 1998

Open hand
take mine

open hand
nail holes
for lifelines

open hand
in the dust

open hand
take mine

nail holes
nail holes
for lifelines

LOST AND FOUND

This morning makes me less
than the night before.
I rolled out of a bed that kept
my name, turned on a light
that failed to recognize me,
looked in a mirror and saw
that I assumed another
man's life, tried to climb back
into bed but found it occupied
by the man who slept there
last night and who was still
fast asleep with a softer looking
version of my face.

I sat at a strange desk
where my knees would not fit
the gap underneath the desk,
held a pen that a leftie, like me,
handled like scissors or a can
opener in a world not meant
for the likes of me.

A SECOND LOOK AS PHYSICIST SLOWS THE SPEED OF LIGHT

In a sequel to Superman, Lois dies
because Superman reaches her too late.
True to form he reverses time
by speeding around the globe
faster than 186,000 miles per second
and succeeds in his second rescue attempt
in saving Lois Lane's life.

Now that light is made to crawl
we are all Superman,
able to save this and that thought
that slipped from our mind
and would not allow itself to be caught.

We can save ourselves from disaster,
slow down the failure of love
long enough to remove ourselves from it,
say something cruel, and, before it settles
in a loved one's ear, take it back.

RIDDLE

I am full of the things single men
take for granted and married ones
dream about, but only the young
at heart really own or can call theirs.

When prodded I curl up like a bud,
millipede or someone thrust into light
after days in a blindfold, or a fist.
And I don't open again, no matter

how long you wait and watch, and no
amount of coaxes and gentle strokes
helps. Do nothing and I am happy.
Say nothing to me and I sing all day.

You see my face but cannot name it.
You'll step over my grave tomorrow.

SCORPIONFLY

You can draw an S
from the top of my head
to the tip of my tail.
There's a sting in my tail
and a tale in my head
about that sting.

Part of me roamed the earth.
Part of me roamed the sky.
And in between these parts of me
roamed earth and sky.

I closed the gap between the two
by joining the top half of the fly
to the bottom half of the scorpion.

It seemed prudent to keep my wings
and keep my sting, to keep my compound
eye that sees all the ways I could use
my sting on an enemy and choose
the most prurient.

My head in the world
A world in my head
The world that's my head
My head for the world.

Would that it were that simple,
that I had two neat halves
and the two were yoked together
merely by my desire.
The fact is my two selves
passed each other every day
for generations without recognizing
their potential united
in one body. The idea of losing
even a crumb of their original selves
seemed tantamount to a slow death
not a metamorphosis to greater things.

And so somewhere between the two
in an Atlantic of the mind
I floated, watched and waited
for the union to happen.

Time passed. An ocean of time.
With each second a drop in the ocean
and each minute a thimbleful of water
laced with salt, and for a day
a bucket full, and one night the same
bucket, three-quarters full,
and a bath of water for a week,
and a small paddling pool for a month,
and a flooded Deptford High Street
for a year; that high street plus a thimbleful
amounts to a leap year.
The capital up to its ankles equals one decade.
A quarter century brings boats into those city
streets for an entire week.
Fifty years of water is all our fears for furniture
and no barrier against it.
A century counts out in lost lives.
A penalty for every stroke on the calendar.
An ocean of sweat and tears;
salt fusing the bones in the inner ear.

Another's head not my head.
Another's body not my body.
My head on another body.
My head but not my body.
My body but not my head.
My head and my body.
Got that?

I have a memory in my tail of another head,
and a memory in my head of another tail.
The two memories meet in my body.
Sometimes they pass each other
along a narrow path in my spinal column
without so much as a howdy or tip of the hat
or nod, as if the engine of each ran on rails
in completely different settings.

The two collided one cool September morning.
I was in mid-flight poised above
fresh droppings from a marsupial
at the moment of that collision.
My tail did not recognize my head
and would have struck and should have struck
but seemed giddy thirty-feet above ground
and connected its fate, its safe landing
to the front part that bore no relation to it
so it stung the air instead, snapped all the air
in my immediate vicinity
out of the atmosphere
creating the equivalent of a vacuum
that caused us both,
by which I mean the whole
package of head and tail with linking body, to fall
several feet before I recovered
our flight but lost my stomach,
in this instance my appetite,
for that trace of fresh marsupial

A compound eye
A compound I
Always sees you.
A compound me
A compound you
In my compound eye
In my compound I.

My tail sees in so far as it feels.
My tail paints what I see
in seven colours adding layers
to the scene until an entire rainbow
defines a crumb already pictured in my head
comprised of multiple sides.

The world is not only gyroscopic,
spinning on its axis with each spin a planet,
as I see it, wrapped around multiple selves
all visible to my eye,
the world sports painted layers of rainbows,
skins of feeling laid one on top of another,
encrusted with colour by my tail.

When I lie down for the night,
when the curve of my tail straightens
and my wings fold,
I sleep with my eyes open.
A lid you can't see drops
over my eyes. A heart I don't have
skips a beat then stops.
My body fills with stillness.
My pores block with the wax of this stillness.
Stillness occupies all ten compartments of my eyes.
Do not try to wake me.
You would be better off trying to erase poverty.

My idea of heaven? Mountains,
valleys and rivers in every conceivable
variety of organic waste matter;
note, not nuclear; it repeats on you.
My idea of hell – disinfected space.

For the wedding of my head and tail
I borrow something from a T-Rex
perfectly preserved;
a sprig from a weeping willow
dipped in a pond;
the bi-focal monocle of a Cyclops;
the tinted pane of glass
off a well in winter;
one lock of those dreads from the Gorgon;
the tip of the black tongue of a Chow;
one second from Roger Bannister;
one medal from Jesse Owens;
one semi-colon from James Joyce;
one brush stroke from Jackson Pollock;
one skip from Mohammed Ali;
one note from Jimi Hendrix;
one look from Marilyn Monroe;
one gesture from Richard Nixon;
one syllable from Martin Luther King;
one sex from Simone de Beauvoir;
one terza rima from Dante;
one regret from Edith Piaf;
one fruit from Billie Holiday;
one windmill from Don Quixote;
one intern from the White House;
one Samurai from the Seven;
one ice cube from the Cold War;
one spark plug from NASA;
one sperm from the sperm whale;
one tube from the Underground;
one more flame from the old flame;

one whisker from Santa's beard;
one nod from the only wink in town;
one wink at the only nod in town;
one town at the Nod and Wink;
one nail in the entire coffin;
one angel on the head of a needle;
one more end to burn on the candle;
one less fingernail on Fu Manchu;
once in a blue moon once more.

SHADOW PLAY

There isn't enough light in the world.
Too many shadows define what I've become
Forcing me to register only those shapes
Shaded from the light and shadowed
By the shade; amorphous, pellucid and cold.
My shadow is sharper than me, and then some:
Ahead, behind or beside me, it takes
Away from me. I'm led by it and not allowed
To forget the fact, unsure when I'll turn
Or stop, or why, afraid that if I sit too long
Or get stuck in a queue, it will walk off
Without me trailing it and never return,
And by the time I notice my shadow gone,
I'll be see-through, insubstantial stuff.

SOUTH SOUTH-EAST

Thunder and lightning capital spare me one banyan root
soaked in mangrove swamp, half-a-cup of razor
grass combed flat by an Atlantic breeze, an alligator tooth.
Grant me a flamingo feather, an iguana toenail, a whisker
from the sleepy manatee, one prismatic scale
from the marlin. Add a sprinkle of what the Florida
panther leaves in its wake for the longest while,
enough to fit between the thumb and index finger.

I pound it, grind it, blend it all up into a paste,
into a pot-pourri, an Everglades morning brew.
I sip it, season my crab and potato stew,
pinch it on rice and eggplant, level it on toast,
feel this country colour my skin and pepper my tongue:
ka-rack, bo-doom, hit me, miss me, weather song.

STORY OF MY SKIN

Canary sing your song
without your feathers and without
dawn for backing vocals.

I listen to you minus my skin
minus the hairs stuck in or drawn out
my skin. I am all ears,

Skinned alive by your song.
I am raw. I am human.
My black skin is a carrier bag;

your bird skin, a tobacco pouch,
or purse for coins and tampax.
Your feathers make a headdress.

Sing for me. I dance for you.
Dance for me. I sing for you.

SONG OF THE TONGUE

Speak in tongues if speak you must
Speak to me while speech is free
So said the wind in the bowed trees
So said the light on the mountain lake

Loosen the forked tongue
Shake it out like a rolled bolt
Of the finest woven cotton

Clothes beaten with wood paddles
By the narrow river or standpipe

The same clothes flap flap flap
On a clothesline strung between
Two fence posts beside the house

That house on stilts and a wind whistling
Through and the tongue loose
In the mouth and free
The swollen tongue moulded by the palate

This mouth this food these days
That the tongue tastes all its life long
This banquet it flaps its way through

How it climbs china cutlery and crystal
At the banquet for tongues

To feast as though walled in
So much so sometimes tongues
Cannot hear themselves think

And all thought amounts to
A tongue cut out and thrown
In a pot and brought in on a platter
For a feast of tongues

WEDNESDAY

If light curves through space
then it moves through time

like my race, in fits and starts,
leaps and bounds, one step

forwards and two backwards,
shining on an eyelid if that eye

shows it favour, painting
behind the eyes, colouring

gums, palms and cuticles.

THE LAST SONNET ABOUT SLAVERY
(After Hogarth)

Put your hand on my shoulder, dear mistress.
Hands as delicate should not hang in the air
But find ample places to pose and rest.
And since my shoulders, my head, the hair
In it, all belong to you, let those hands
Settle anywhere on me, but do not let them float
Aimlessly, nor be idle, nor stand
Out as if they had no greater goal.

Hands that don't know the scrubbing brush,
Or weight of any thing, other than a necklace
Or dress, stocking or shift that they adjust
Are not hands, but butterflies on a leash.
Let them wave and dart if you must, but please,
When they settle, let their good luck fall on me.

ACKNOWLEDGEMENTS

These poems are selected from *Mama Dot* (Chatto, 1985), *Airy Hall* (Chatto, 1989), *British Subjects* (Bloodaxe, 1993) and *Bill of Rights* (Chatto, 1998). The poem 'Granny on Her Singer Sewing Machine' is taken from the script of the play *A Jamaican Airman Foresees His Death* in *Black Plays 3* (Methuen, 1995). The poems have also appeared in *Ariel*, *The Bloodaxe Book of Caribbean Poetry*, ed. E. A. Markham (Bloodaxe, 1989), *Callaloo*, *Cambridge Review*, *Concert of Voices*, ed. Victor J. Ramraj (Broadview, 1998), *First and Always* (Faber & Faber, 1989), *Independent*, *Independent on Sunday*, *Jacaranda Review*, *Landfall*, *Leave to Stay*, ed. Joan Riley and Brian Wood (Virago, 1996), *London Review of Books*, *Mangrove*, *Massachusetts Review*, *News For Babylon*, ed. James Berry (Chatto, 1984), *New Writing 1* (Minerva, 1992), *The Penguin Book of Caribbean Poetry* (Penguin, 1986), *Pivot*, *The Poetry Book Society Anthology* (1985 and 1986/7), *Poetry Review*, *Quarry*, *Race Today*, *Salt*, *Soho Square* (Bloomsbury, 1988), *Stand*, *Wasafiri*. In addition some of the poems have been broadcast on *Nightwaves* (BBC Radio 3) and *Kaleidoscope* (BBC Radio 4). Parts of poems from the film *Sweet Thames* (directed by Mark Harrison for the BBC 'Words on Film' series, produced by Peter Symes, and shown on BBC 2 in March 1992) appear in revised form.

The author and publisher would like to thank Bloodaxe for permission to reproduce the poems from *British Subjects*.